Stephanie J. Ford

Preface

Life is about taking chances. If we always do what we have always done, we will get what we have already become.

Every day, wake up and strive to be the best you that you can be. Learn to never give up and to keep your eye on the prize.

There aren't any failures in life, just opportunities to improve yourself before the next journey. Successful people live life on purpose and have usually failed several times before they made their first million.

Keep a winning attitude.

YOU WILL ALWAYS BE A WINNER!

Dedicated to my parents. She-Vestor
would not exist without them

Contents

She-Vestor™

*A female investor who puts money into
financial plans, stocks, property, etc with
the expectation of achieving a profit*

Welcome to the Boys' Club: A She-Vestor™ is Born

Let me be the first to say that breaking into this field definitely wasn't easy. For years, I was seen as the typical woman who probably didn't know anything about investing. However, I graduated at the top of my class in high school with a 3.7 GPA and got a degree in Electrical and Computer Engineering, so I'm definitely not your average woman.

My real estate career has allowed me to learn a lot from my male investors. While showing investment properties, my male investors taught me the "tricks of the trade" so to speak. After spending time with them, I was able to estimate how much renovation costs a house would take; what deficiencies were present; how to estimate the types and costs of materials needed and how to negotiate with sub-contractors. So, they let me in on the boys' club, not realizing that one day I would join them. This knowledge has been a highly valuable tool to have. It has helped me in negotiations with sellers when making offers and knowing when to walk away. I am not emotionally tied to any property. They are all just transactions. If the numbers don't work, then they just don't work.

Often, when I go view a property and I meet a potential seller, they ask me where my husband is. I laugh and say I'm not married. Then they look surprised. After I view the property, I let them know that I will get back to them after I consult with my "partner". Even though I have the final say in any acquisition, I often times will consult with my foreman and property manager on some property purchases. Then I will do a second inspection with them present, just to make sure that I didn't miss anything the first time around. You will find out that a lot of time you do.

This boys' club has its advantages and disadvantages. At Lowes I get preferred treatment when I walk in the door. Maybe it's because they know

I'm coming to spend a lot of money. At one store, I am recognized as the store's top customer. At this store, I get free delivery and my orders get to jump to the front of the line when placed. A big disadvantage is that some of the male subcontractors will "try" to take advantage of me, thinking that I don't know the game or that I don't know what I'm doing. That never goes very far. I let them finish telling me their thoughts. Then I let them know how things should be handled and they look surprised. At that point, we have an understanding… and that's if I decide to proceed with their business at all.

This boys' club also led me to get my homebuilder's license. I'm in a male-dominated world in every spectrum and I love it. I bought my first pair of steel-toe boots last year because I was at a job site and I stepped on a nail. It only took one time of feeling that nail in my foot and I promised myself that it would not happen again. That night I went straight to the store and got not one, but two pairs of steel toe boots. After the boots come off, I am back to being regular Diva Stephanie. That part of me will never go away.

Now I'm going to show you how I took what I learned and how I made $90,000 in four months of flipping houses. This didn't include my other income. It was just my bonus money. I know normally authors will explain how to achieve something first, then give you case studies. However, I'm going to do it in reverse. I want to get you excited about the possibility of what can be achieved, then I will explain how to do it.

Let's go!!!

Fail First,
Then Try Again

ust remember that, when you start off, it is never all roses. In 2006, long before I started making what I would call "big" money, I decided I was going to "flip" a house. Well, I was still a newbie in real estate and I thought I knew what I was doing. I did everything wrong that I could have. I paid too much for the house. I bought it in a bad location. It had a horrible floor plan. Most of all I spent too much money on the renovations. In order to get out of this ordeal that I had created, I rented the property so I could pay the mortgage payments. At this point, I figured I could breathe a little. This lasted for about six months until the renters got behind and I couldn't afford to make the payments. Next step was either a foreclosure or short sale. Since I knew that the financial impact of a short sale was better than a foreclosure, I chose that option. My credit did take a hit, but since I had just bought my home that I planned to stay in and I had a decent vehicle to drive, I didn't worry about it too much.

Fast forward to 2020, the year of the pandemic. How can we forget? This was the Great Depression all over again. This year was definitely not for the faint at heart. The rate of job losses was unbelievable. Business owners suffered the worst. The government bailout offered some initial relief but honestly, it was a Band-Aid compared to the revenue lost during this time. I sat at home for two months like most people, wondering how I was going to make it. I contacted all my creditors to get payment extensions because my money had stopped. Every day I was praying for a breakthrough or a miracle.

In May, my construction business picked back up so my income was back. I took what I had and started working on a plan of action. It took me two months to get it together but I finally did. I took a chance and enrolled in a coaching plan for property investors. It cost me $1,000. I soon learned how to find motivated sellers and implemented a plan to start making me some money.

The next thing I did was to contact a mailing company and signed up for three mailing campaigns which cost me $8,000. That was a lot of money for someone that had just started back working. I felt that I really didn't have a choice. My entire career has been built on faith so I couldn't turn back now. Matthew 17:20 says "If ye have faith as a grain of mustard seed, ye shall say unto this mountain, Remove hence to yonder place; and it shall remove; and nothing shall be impossible unto you." I stood on God's Word and didn't look back.

Case Study 1

My first mailing campaign went out in mid June 2020. If you have never done this before, it is the most nerve-wracking thing ever! You are wondering every day if the phone is going to ring knowing that, if it does, this could potentially be the phone call that pushes you into the next tax bracket. So, as I was patiently waiting and waiting, I finally got my first phone call.

"Hi, this is Stephanie."

"I'm calling about a postcard that you sent me"

"Yes ma'am?"

"Take me off your mailing list and my house is not for sale."

(Caller hangs up)

So, now I was holding the phone feeling kind of devastated.

Then there was a second phone call. (This time my answering service picked it up)

"Do not send me anymore of your ridiculous post-cards and take me off your mailing list."

OK, so I go through this about eight more times and then I get the golden phone call.

"Is this Stephanie Ford?"

Yes, it is.

"I'm going to make you a deal of a lifetime."

"You are?" (At this point, I'm grinning from ear to ear) "Sir, what is it?"

"I'm going to sell you a house worth $150,000 and all I want is $15,000!"

"$15,000. Are you serious?"

I was staring at the phone, thinking, "Wow, these cards really work!" So, I dropped what I was doing and rushed out to the property to see what I was about to acquire.

When I got to the property according to the GPS, all I saw was a lot of overgrown brush. So, I drove back and forth a few times to double check the address. Then I decided to call the owner.

"Hello, sir it's Stephanie. I'm at your property in Mulga and wanted to double check that I had the address right."

"Yes, it's... 123 Street, Mulga, AL."

"OK, sir. I was just double checking the address because I don't see a house. All I see is a lot. There is no house."

"Stephanie, there is a house. The grass just needs to be cut."

At this point, I'm sitting in my truck confused because I still cannot make out a house behind this tall grass.

"Sir when can you get someone to cut the grass for me to view the property?"

"I don't know… maybe in the next month or two. But you can cut the grass if you like."

Now at this point, I was thinking I wasn't going to be cutting anyone's grass for them. On the other hand, if I was about to make a pretty penny, why not?

I went home and called one of my contacts and asked them to meet me at the house. They got there before me and had gone through the house and taken pictures. It turned out to be a complete dump and tear down. The back of the house was gone, one side had water damage and the floor and roof had caved in.

So, me still being Ms. Optimistic, thinking I could do this and make some money, I decided to go back to the seller and offer him $10,000. He said no to that offer but we settled on $12,000. At this point, I was still feeling good because there was a $200,000 house sitting across the street. After title came back, I realize that the seller had obtained the property by a quit claim deed and not a general warranty deed. This was a bummer as it meant I would have to quiet title if I wanted to sell the property to a regular buyer. So, I backed out the contract.

Since you might not be familiar with these terms, let me explain. A quit claim deed, gives you rights to the property however often times you cannot secure title insurance. This is because a warranty can only be set in place from the date of closing and not before. A general warranty deed is often obtained in 90% of real estate transactions. A general warranty deed allows you to obtain title insurance in which you have a warranty of before, during and after you own the property. In order to convert a quit claim deed to a general warranty deed, a quiet action suite must be file in which it releases any claims against the property.

So, I bet you are thinking, what's wrong with quieting title and picking up this property for $12,000? Nothing is wrong with quieting title, but after my experience with my previous flip in 2006, I didn't want my next flip to be this one. On this particular property, there was no chain of title so there was no telling how long it would be before I could get clear title.

This was the only promising lead that came of the first mailing campaign, so I was a little disappointed. But that meant it was time to go back to the drawing board and try again. I changed my mailer for the second campaign and hoped for better results.

Case Study 2

The mailers went out for the second campaign in July 2020. This time I added a texting option to my mailer. This cost me a little more money, but I was on a mission. I received about thirty text responses and fifteen phone calls from about 4,000 mailouts. I thought this was a pretty good result compared to the previous mailer. I got some great leads this time. I went under contract with two properties and canceled one. I bought a property for $28,000. It was a nice three-bedroom, two bath house in Bessemer, AL. I resold the property to one of my investors for $38,500. Since I am a contractor, I also did the rehab and later rented the property for him. We still manage the property in our portfolio. Now, I bet you are wondering why didn't I keep the property. Honestly, I wasn't yet ready to take on rental properties of my own. I was trying to build capital, plus I felt I had a great business model. I would find the property, rehab it, then manage the property. So instead of making money one time, I'm making money three times. And the third way enabled me to bring in residual income each month. The immediate profit from this one property paid for the mailing campaigns and the coaching program.

Coaching Program $1,000
Mailing Budget $8,000
Profit after Sale: $10,500
Net Profit: $1,500 (I'm not counting my rehab money but of course there was profit there too.)

The money made from property one gave me the confidence to push harder and keep going. It was time to move on to property two.

An investor that I had become friends with had decided to invest in Birmingham. He bought a package of properties from another seller who was ready to clean house. Well, of course, he didn't want to keep all the properties that he had bought, so he offered some to me. I purchased one of his proper-ties for $36,000. I was torn about whether to keep it or not, but in the end, I decided to sell it. I sold it for $45,000 to one of my hedge fund investors, making $9,000 in less than thirty days in the process.

What I want to teach you about now is the importance of building relationships. I have built several relationships over the years. You cannot be taught to build this type of network in a book; it's something that you have to learn in life. Have you ever wondered why, when a property goes on the market, it's instantly under contract? Well, think about it. It's because the Realtor already had a buyer and wrote the contract at the same time as the listing was put in the MLS. It's all about relationships in this business. Over the years I have built numerous relationships with different investors. My business could not survive without them. If you remember nothing else from this book, please remember that you have to have relationships if you want to last in this business.

Case Study 3

The third mailing campaign was also sent out in July 2020, almost concurrently with the second, meaning that the mailers overlapped. They were only a few weeks apart. But like I said earlier, I was on a mission. This time, I got a call from a nice older gentleman who was very persistent about me returning his phone call. This time I was able to purchase a duplex for $12,500. However, things were not all peaches and cream when it came to obtaining it. There was a squatter that we had to get out before we took possession. This guy was a character. He would leave the house and call his friend to house sit so that we couldn't come in and change the locks. Well, this went on for thirty days until we boarded the windows and changed the locks. This was all with the owner's permission, of course. When I finally closed on the house, I had already found another duplex that I liked more, so guess what; I sold it for $26,500. Yes, I made $14,000!

This property came at the end of a thirty-day period for me. In thirty days, I had purchased three properties, done absolutely no rehab and made $33,500. Imagine making this type of money in thirty days. At this point, you feel like you're on top of the world and you can do anything.

I told you that the second and third campaigns ran almost concurrently. From campaign three, I had two sellers contact me. One was the owner of an occupied duplex and the other was the owner of an occupied quadplex. Honestly, the owner of the duplex gave me the run around; they had a friend that they wanted to give first shot at the property to, and I was a nobody. I didn't give up on that property. I just put it on the back of my stack at the time. In the meantime, I received a voicemail from the owner of the quadplex. I did a drive by but I decided not to call him back because I thought the property was a single-family house. Honestly the property looked like an old abandoned house that needed a lot of work and I really didn't want to deal with anything like that. Little did I know what treasure I was passing up.

I stayed persistent with the owner of the duplex. In the end, I had to think outside the box. I sent them an offer to purchase their property with an expiration date. Well honestly, I didn't know if that was going to work or not. I hadn't been taught to do this or ever tried it before but life is all about taking chances, right? The night before the expiration date, I received a phone call.

"Hi Stephanie, this is Susan. I've been meaning to call you."

"Hi Susan."

"I received your letter. Is this offer still valid?"

"Yes, it is."

"Can I have more time to make a decision?"

"No, I sent out several offers and my funds are limited so the quicker you make a decision the better."

"OK Stephanie, let me talk to my husband and I will contact you tomorrow."

"Thanks Susan!"

Susan called me the next day as promised and we set an appointment to see the property, after which I signed the contract at $26,000. Now this one was really a sweet deal because the duplex was occupied, with tenants paying $295 per month each. I knew the rent was low, but I didn't care, because I was going to renovate it and raise it anyway.

While I stayed persistent with the owner of the duplex, the owner of the quadplex stayed persistent with me. He called me again so I returned his phone call the second time and he told me that the property was a quadplex and that it was currently used as a boarding house. There were two tenants paying him $265 per week and he was ready to move on and sell the property. After numerous conversations, he told me he wanted $20,000. Even though there was money to be made, I thought that it was still a little high with the amount of work needed so I made him an offer of $12,000. After a week, we settled at $15,000.

Due to my main objective being buying and selling, I sold the property to one of my investors for $32,500. I closed on the quadplex first at $15,000, then sold it to one of my investors for $32,500, making $17,500. I took that $17,500 and put it toward the $26,000 I needed to purchase the duplex. So now, instead of me taking $26,000 out of my account, I only had to transfer $9,500 to make this purchase. What a wonderful world!

I immediately started with renovations on the duplex because I was going to flip it. After all was said and done, I spent $22,000. I managed to sell it to one of my investors for $79,000 before the renovations were complete. On this flip I made $31,000, allowing for the costs of the renovations.

I gave this investor a discount because he was buying another of my properties that I had recently contracted from my mailings. On that purchase, I made $8,000.

So, let's recap.

I initially spent:
$1,000 on a coaching program
$8,000 on mailouts

Then I made
$10,500 from property one
$9,000 from property two (not from mailouts but
    from my sphere of influence)
$14,000 from property three
$17,500 from property four
$31,000 from property five
$8,000 from property six
Which totals $90,000.

In addition, I made money through property management and renovations on properties one, four, and six. And all this was from a $9,000 investment. I ended the year 2020 with $90,000 more in my bank account. This was the motivation that helped me start the year 2021 off successfully.

HOW YOU START IS NEVER HOW YOU FINISH

Motivation

ow! $90,000 in four months! Hey, that was all working part-time with very little effort. Just think how it could have been if I had multiplied my efforts and gone full throttle. I would be too hard to handle. So that's what I decided that I was going to do when it came to my investment business. After all, everything goes hand in hand anyway. I am still a full-time real estate broker but honestly, I spend more time investing and renovating properties than being an agent. I have more freedom this way and it gives me more flexibility. These days, it's about working smarter, not harder. I'm still grateful that I had been informally inducted into the boys' club because without that, I wouldn't be where I am today.

So here I am doing it again and this time I have picked up two properties so far with a potential return of $70,000 in forty-five days. Paydays like this make life a lot easier. At this point, most people say that I can sit down for the rest of the year and relax. Honestly, that's the worst thing that you can do. You can afford to relax a little bit, but not too much, because you have to keep going until you get to your comfort zone and I'm not there yet. It's hard to keep the same lifestyle by relaxing every time you get a big paycheck. In the commission world, you must keep going because you never know when things will slow down and you will have to live off your savings.

So, how do you do it?
Here's the secret...

Step 1: Research
Step 2: Take Action
Step 3: Implement
Step 4: Repeat and Reinvest in your Business

Why Invest in Real Estate?

re you wondering if now is the right time for you invest in real estate? Real estate is the one industry that never dies. People are born and people die every day. This keeps the real estate cycle going because we have to have a place to live. When people die properties are normally sold through estate sales. When people fall behind on their mortgage, foreclosures happen. This opens the door to bank auctions. People are not paying property taxes which opens opportunities for tax deed acquisitions for investors. Married couples are getting divorced. Therefore, the judge orders the marital property to be sold as a result of the divorce decree.

When the pandemic started in 2020, the real estate market boomed while other industries plummeted.

Buyers took advantage of low interest rates while sellers took advantage of high property values. It was a win-win for everyone.

According to the national average there are over 1.4 million vacant homes in the United States today. Imagine the possibilities of potential income if you had a fraction of these vacant homes as rental or flip properties. The housing demand for single family income rentals has grown since the pandemic last year in 2020.

The media claims that we have a housing shortage. To a certain extent we do. However, the average person doesn't know where to find inventory. Houses are still being purchased in this "national housing crisis" as it is called now. However, they are being purchased off market. Very few houses are making it to the market to be available to the public. The properties are being sold in private, directly from seller to purchaser. Realtors used to be the source for finding properties but now they are the least likely source of finding the best properties for an investor. So, in order for you to stay two steps ahead of the game, you must learn how to find off market properties yourself or have a really good source.

THE RIGHT ACQUISITION IS KEY IN ANY PROPERTY INVESTMENT

Take Off Running

Getting Started

If you are thinking about investing in real estate you have to begin with the end in mind. Then most importantly, you have to get started. The next three steps will help you to begin.

Step 1
WAKE UP AND GET DRESSED!

After being self-employed for eighteen years this is one very important part of my day. I have realized that even if you work from home, you have to act as though someone is going to see you. The reason is that, if you get dressed and prepare your work space, you get yourself into a different frame of mind. Let's say you get the call of a lifetime to see a property that you have had your eye on: Well, you can't go if you are still in your PJs. I know this next thing I'm going to say might seem elementary, but brush your teeth and eat breakfast. It's a proven fact that you will have a better conversation once you have a fresh mouth and have put something in your stomach or at least had your morning coffee. Just try it and let me know how it goes.

Step 2
SET A GOAL

What do you want to achieve in real estate?

Do you want to be a millionaire Realtor or do you want to be an investor? Honestly most people just want to make money. After being a Realtor for five years, I quickly learned that this business was not enough for me. However, I stayed in it because it paid the bills and honestly, I was good at it. If you really knew me, you would have seen me doing something new every few years, because I knew this is not where I was going to end up. Instead, I kept exploring different areas until I found one I could see myself retiring from.

When I became licensed in 2003, I always knew that I wouldn't be in traditional real estate very long. However, I didn't know when that time period would end. So, here I am eighteen years later and the wave has finally come. Six years after I got my license, I started working more intensively with investors, after the real estate crash of 2007. During this time, I became very familiar with design and construction. Even though I didn't hold a contractor's license at the time, I spent a lot of time on the job site with the contractors and they familiarized me with the process. This enabled me to add more experience to my resume, and soon I became a construction manager. My clients, who were out of state investors, asked me to oversee their projects to make sure things were going according to their specifications with their contractor. I was responsible for paying the contractors. Now, of course, I did this all for free. I had no idea that this could be a real paying job. However, I initially sold the property to the investor and would then be the one to list the property when the renovations were finished, so there was an upside. And while I did a lot of free work, it allowed me to gain a wealth of knowledge.

At that time, my heart was still in being an awesome Realtor. Changing over to being an investor never crossed my mind. I was making $150,000+ in my real estate career so life was good.

Let me give you the pros and cons of being a Realtor as opposed to an investor.

Realtor:

Pro: You make additional income by selling properties for a commission.

Con: You are bound by License Law.

Yes, when you are a Realtor, you must follow the law exactly or you stand the chance of losing your main source of income. A lot of Realtors get sloppy and careless, and forget the risk they are taking when it comes to this. So, if you are an investor now, don't get your license. It's just not worth it.

Investor:

Pro: You can do whatever you want; just make sure you don't do anything that will get you jail time.

Con: No direct access to MLS but who cares?

In my early years in real estate, a Realtor, mortgage broker, investor, and attorney I knew all went to jail for mortgage fraud. They were buying properties, setting up fake buyers and mortgages and cashing out on the properties. I guess they were crazy enough to think that they wouldn't get caught. Of course, everyone involved got jail time and the Realtor, mortgage broker, and attorney lost their professional licenses. Some things are just not worth it.

Step 3
DESIGN YOUR ROAD TO SUCCESS

One of the things I have been stressing is the importance of building relationships. You can't get anywhere in this business without getting to know people. A lot of times, deals are made with a handshake, a phone call, over lunch, or during a night out on the town. Yes, it's all about networking. So, who do you know?

I currently have several people in my network that I can call personally. These are people that I can sell properties to, get loans from, enter joint ventures with, and so on. This network is more valuable than any type of schooling. This is what makes the world go around.

Part of your job as an investor is always trying to find the next deal. If you have no properties, then you can't make any money. Being a Realtor doesn't cut it for finding inventory. Actually, being a Realtor is honestly the worst job you can have when it comes to finding inventory because none of this is taught to you. I don't have to find inventory when I have my license; all I have to do is sit back and wait for someone to call to sell a house or go look for it on the MLS.

When you are an investor it's different. You have no MLS. You may have a relationship with a Realtor who can access the MLS for you, but again it's only limited to what they can find. Let's face it, most Realtors are lazy and really don't want to work that hard. Why should they when they can make $6,000 selling a house for $200,000 for maybe two to eight hours of their time? Hey, that's a great income if that's all you want.

Now let's talk about the real money! After I invested the initial $1,000, I invested another $1,500 to teach me how to virtual wholesale (selling properties from another state), then I took another $5,000 coaching program and enrolled in another inves-tor platform for $3,000. So overall, I spent $10,500 in nine months. I was investing in myself to get me to where I wanted to be. Before you become an expert, first you must become a student. I never had a problem with learning. Remember, knowledge is power.

What did I get for this $10,500?

- I can find all vacant houses nationwide.
- I can find all houses in pre-foreclosure.
- I can find if an owner is upside on their mortgage.
- I can perform skip trace operations by finding the owner's current mailing address, phone number and email address.
- I have learned multiple techniques for contacting motivated sellers.
- Most of all, I have learned to be financially free forever.

Now, before we go on, I am not selling anything. I am just giving you knowledge and guiding you to get started like I did.

If you are wondering what coaching program to use, just remember to use someone with a proven track record and definitely not someone whose only method is Facebook advertising. Make sure you google the company and see if they are a member of the BBB. This is what I did each time I enrolled into a course. I am a member myself now.

Now that you have the keys to success, it's time to implement them.

SUCCESS LIES IN THE HANDS OF THOSE WHO WANT IT

Implementation Time

1. Set Your Budget

How much money are you willing to invest in yourself? This is the million-dollar question. You might think that you can't afford to risk anything at this moment. If that's how you feel, then that's actually why you need to run and do it fast. When I knew that I needed to make a change but I didn't have as much money as I thought I needed, I invested what I had. When I made my first sale, I reinvested that money so that I could make more money, then I repeated the cycle. Please don't take your mortgage or car note money to invest in marketing; remember you still have to have a place to live and a vehicle to drive. I just don't want you to be scared to take chances that will help you to make changes in your life. Please remember that nothing in life is guaranteed, but keep in mind that being afraid will never get you anywhere. Always remember that the risk you take is the one that could change your life.

Plan on a minimum of three to six months to generate a consistent lead flow. Sometimes you might hit a home run with the first try but sometimes you won't.

2. Define Your Area

Do you want to market where you live, or do you want to break into another area? Once you decide on your area, break it down into county, city and/or zip code. Get to know the area code types in real estate.

A area — This is the best of the best. It has the best school system; the highest property value; and the highest resale value. These are your A paper clients. The areas are usually where the corporate owners live. Here you will find doctors, attorneys, business owners, country club members, "old" money, and so on. This will be a high rent district; over $500k in value.

B area — This is still similar to A, however this group had to earn their way to the status quo; it wasn't handed down to them. This area is close to the A area but not in the A area. You will still find doctors, attorneys, business owners, CEOs, but definitely not old money. The school district is still comparable but maybe not the best. This will be a medium to high rent district; $250k–$500k in value.

C area — This is your working class group. Nothing at all was handed to this group, but it is a college educated group that works nine to five. The school system might not be the best but that's OK because the parents that can afford it will send their children to private school. This will be a medium rent district; $80k–$250k in value.

D/F area — This is normally the warzone. It is the worst of the worst. The property values are extremely low and the school district is less than stellar. Here you will find several areas of government housing and several types of public transportation. This group usually doesn't have cars and relies on public assistance. This will be a very low rent district; below $60k in value.

The type of area will determine how much you should pay for your property. This guide should help you. It is OK to combine the areas within your portfolio, so long as you know what you are doing. Often, I will have investors ask for a BC or a CD area. That lets me know that they want something in between so that's what I aim for.

3. Decide On Your Search Criteria

It is extremely important to know what type of property you are looking for before you start searching. If you don't define your search criteria then you will be going in circles.

- What age property are you looking for?
- What square footage?
- What is the minimum and maximum number of bedrooms and baths?
- Do you want the owners to be located in state or out of state?
- Are you targeting banks or just regular homeowners?
- Are you looking for vacant properties?
- Are you looking for properties in foreclosure?
- Are you looking for properties in probate?
- Do you want to target divorced homeowners?

- Do you want expired listings?
- Do you want aged properties (which have spent more than ninety days on the market)?

4. Campaign Type

Direct Mail Campaign

There are companies that have pre-formatted post-cards and letters for motivated sellers. All you have to do is send them your list and they will do all the work for you. I found that a texting option added to the postcards worked well for me because, when the homeowner texted a code, all of their information was automatically sent to my email, so I was able to review it before I called them back.

Ringless Voice Mail Drops

This can be a bit expensive, but it sure beats cold calling. You can leave a pre-recorded message that will either go to your voicemail or, if they are interested, the voicemail will do a live transfer. Live transfers are great because, if someone really is ready to sell, then you will want to speak to them right away. The additional money is definitely worth it.

Text Messages

This method is very cost effective. Sometimes you can run campaigns for as little as $0.02 per message. You can also set up automatic text responses, so you won't miss any opportunities when the homeowners call back. There are several companies that offer both ringless voicemail drops and text messages. One thing to look for is to make sure that they scrub the do not call registry. Also, you want a second phone number for your outbound calls and text messages. Most companies will assist you with that.

Email Campaigns

If you use this method, make sure you use a program with an unsubscribe link, so your email address won't get blacklisted. It is always a good idea to set up another email address just for the mailing list. Also set up several IP addresses.

It will be necessary to try any of the above methods several times to get the results that you want. You will sometimes have to mail the same people as many as three to six times before they respond. The same goes for emails and text messages. Timing can play a big part as well. When the time is right, it doesn't matter how many mailers they have got previously, you are just the lucky one that was in the right place at the right time.

5. Other Methods of Advertising

Bandit Signs

I'm sure you have seen the "WE BUY HOUSES" signs on the road. These signs do really work. If people are looking for a buyer, they will call. The only thing about this is that they are time-consuming to put out and they will probably get pulled up every week so you do have to replenish your supply.

Billboards

This is another effective way to reach mass quantities. Billboards are excellent advertising because you are not just targeting a specific list, but you are also reaching a large number of people that will pass along your information when they see the advertisement. You can choose stationary or digital billboards. The higher the visibility the better for you.

Google

Google advertising can get expensive but who doesn't use Google? First, set up your Google business page. Then set up keyword searches to drive traffic to your website by creating an ad. This will really pay off in the long run and will help your SEO results.

Social Media Campaigns

If you are going to be in business, act like a business, and set up a Facebook business page. Some people advertise on their personal Facebook page, but the truth is that people don't want to celebrate your business ventures with you. Have you ever noticed that if you post a picture, a joke or something crazy you get 500 likes or comments, but when you post you started a business you hear crickets...? Yeah, most people don't want to celebrate you making money, so get a business page then invite people to like your page. The people that want to follow you will follow you and those that don't want to won't. Then start putting interesting content on your page so that people will share the content; this way you will get free advertising. One of the best things about a business page is that you can boost your page to the entire social media network with paid advertising. Now you can reach thousands of people and tell them about your services.

Craigslist

Craigslist is the forgotten advertisement method. The reason is that most people associate it with scams, which Is far from the truth. I have run ads for "WE BUY HOUSES ANY CONDITION, ANYWHERE" and have gotten several good leads from them. The only thing about this is that you have to stay in front of the line by renewing the ad regularly. If you run this ad, you will have people contacting you from all over the place. One time last year, I picked up a $10 million client looking for apartment complexes from an ad that I ran on my mission quest. I haven't sold him anything yet, but I have written several offers for him. The highest offer so far has been $19 million dollars. Oh boy, that would have been a nice payday, if that had gone through! It's just a matter of time before we get an offer to go to contract, though.

Word of Mouth

Do you have business cards? If not, get some. How do you expect people to know you are in business if you don't advertise yourself? Closed mouths don't get fed. When I decided I was going to start invest-ing, I got 500 business cards and 500 note cards made by Vistaprint. That way, when I passed a bul-letin board or met someone in the street, I could give them my information. Often, when I go to look at properties, strangers come up to me and ask me if I buy houses. I say "Yes, let me give you my card." Well, this has obviously worked because I now get calls, emails and text messages from com-plete strangers telling me that they have heard that I buy houses, and they have a property that they want to sell. Then I smile and see if I can make the deal work for me.

Driving For Dollars

Have you ever passed by a house and wondered what the address was or how you can find the owner's information? There is an app that you can down-load called Driving for Dollars. It is the easiest way to find the missing information on that property address. It gives you the owner's mailing address, phone number, and sometimes the email address. Also, if you have several properties to check, you can export the list. This is a valuable tool to have.

6. Determine Your System

Systems are extremely important during the early phases. How are you going to handle the incoming phone calls? Do you have an assistant, or will you handle all the calls yourself? This needs to be decided before the first mailer goes out, the first business card is passed out or the first ad is placed.

Make sure you have a list of questions to pre-qualify and/or pre-screen the homeowner when you speak to them. Flying by the seat of your pants can lead to you losing the lead. If they don't give you the answer you want, ask their permission to follow up with them in a few months. Most of the time, they will agree to allow you to call back.

Find out how motivated they are to sell. During the conversation, your job is to listen and hear what they are saying. If you listen carefully then you will be able to identify their hot buttons and what will push them to go to contract with you. Bear in mind that they are calling you for a reason; they are not just curious. If they were just curious, they would not have called the number. Your job is to keep them on the phone and to find their hot spots. You have to get an appointment. Most people want you to just give them a number but let them know that a blind number would really be unfair to them. If you are in town, try to make it your business to see the property in person. While you are on the phone with them, try to look up the tax records and do a Google map search to see what you are working with and if this might be worth your time. One thing that I always do is say, "Sorry I'm in the middle of a meeting right now, so can I take your information and call you back when I'm finished?" That way I have plenty of time to do my research before I call them back.

Just today, I received five calls from a mail campaign that I sent out two weeks ago. One of them came from a lady in Huntsville. She started the conversation with "I received your card and I wanted to know what offer you had in mind." Once she told me her address, I started to look up her tax records while making small talk with her. During this time, she told me how she had bought the property for her grandson who planned on renovating the property but he had done nothing with it for years. Then she told me that there had been several break-ins (which is not uncommon for a vacant house) and that she was just tired of it and ready to sell. I saw that she had purchased the property for $16,000 four years ago, so I offered her $15,000. She said no. Then I asked her what would she be willing to take. Her response was more than what I paid for it. She told me that the tax value was $40,000. So I said, "According to your tax records, you paid $16,000 in 2017." She replied "Ma'am that's wrong, I paid $18,000 and I won't take less than $19,000." So, I said great, let's make an appointment so I can view the property." I know that the area that the house is in is a hot area right now and I can get more than $19,000 on a flip or, if I keep it as a rental, I will generate $900 per month. Now, if I get to the property and there is more damage than I anticipated, I can always talk her down on site. But the key is to get my foot in the door.

7. Take Notes and Smile When Speaking

Do you know that when you smile, your tone of voice is different? My sister often laughs when she's around me when I answer a business call because I have my "business" voice on. She'll say "Whoa, I almost didn't recognize you." I reply "Honey, it's about making that money." In the same way, it is important to make small talk. Ask the prospect about their day, talk about the weather, or whatever.

Things like that will lighten the mood. And don't forget to take notes: you may think you will be able to remember the key points, but it's best to note them down immediately.

8. Follow Up

Follow up is key in any business. How many times do you think major inventors got turned down before they got a yes? The best salespeople keep trying and don't take no as a no. Instead, they take no as a not right now. That's why you keep sending out the postcards or you keep calling every few months. Maybe the timing wasn't right when you first had the conversation with them, or maybe something came up that was more important. Don't get discouraged. Keep pushing along and keep them on your list. Most people will give up. Just think if I had given up on the owner who sold me the occupied duplex; then I wouldn't have had the chance to make $31,000 and gain a new client. So, follow up and persistence makes a difference.

Fix and Flip vs Buy and Hold

There are many times when, before considering purchasing properties, an investor has to decide on a strategy, in particular whether to flip the property or to retain the property as a rental. It's not a decision to be taken lightly because, while flipping a property can make you quick money, holding the property and keeping it as a rental can make you long term money. The end result depends on your goals and exit strategy.

Fix and Flip

Advantages

1. You have the potential to make a quick return. In most cases you will flip the property in three to six months.
2. The ARV (after repair value) is based on what the market has done in the previous six to twelve months and most likely won't change too drastically.
3. Because you most likely will be selling to a retail buyer, you can play with the volatility of the market and get the best price possible.
4. After you sell the property, you will have money to reinvest into your next property or put into your pocket.
5. Here you get a chance to introduce your creative eye to the real estate world. Once you flip a few, then people will know about your design skills.
6. You can write off the expenses of the renovation project.

Disadvantages

1. Anything can come up at any instant on a fix and flip which will ruin your chances for that huge return.
2. First time investors tend to "over" renovate and kill their budget because they design it as though they are moving there themselves.
3. If you have got a hard money loan, the interest-only payments may be coming to an end, and you may be forced to sell for less than you wanted because you can't afford the upcoming principal and interest payments.
4. Your contract will be at the mercy at an appraiser if you accept a financed contract.
5. Your property might not sell as fast as you want it to, in which case you may be forced to rent it or give it back to the bank if you have a loan.
6. It might take two or three contracts before the property is sold, by which time your profit margin will have narrowed.
7. You will pay taxes on your earnings.

Buy and Hold

Advantages

1. Long term income. It is a proven fact that most renters continue to rent for ten to thirty years or more. If you are that lucky, just think how much money you will have made.
2. You can pay a little less for rental properties because you don't necessarily care about the ARV.
3. You can put fewer quality finishes in rentals because you are renting, not selling.
4. Once you rehab the property you can take out a mortgage to pull your cash out and purchase other properties.
5. If you own the property free and clear you have equity.
6. You have a tax write-off each year.

Disadvantages

1. You have to pay for all repairs when items break down.
2. Tenants might not pay, and you will have pay to get them evicted.
3. You have to pay the property taxes each year.

4. Your property might sit vacant for months before it's rented to the next tenant.
5. Repair costs can exceed the incoming rent.
6. Tenants might damage the property on purpose or through negligence.
7. The property value might decrease and you might have to sell for less than you paid for it.

As you can see, there are advantages and disadvantages to each option. The path you take will depend on your short-and long-term financial goals. Some investors decide to flip properties to take care of debts now so that they can afford to buy and hold properties for long term income later on. Other investors flip properties for income purposes because this is their main stream of income. On the other hand, there are out of state investors who buy properties nationwide to build up a retirement income for when they stop working. These investors have very little involvement in the process. They hire a team to manage everything for them and collect their rent check every month. So, if you want to be this type of investor, make sure that you have a property manager, Realtor, contractor and attorney in place to handle your affairs.

Cash, Finance or Private Money Funds (Hard Money)

Cash

'm sure you have always heard cash is king and it is. Cash is so much easier to deal with. But unfortunately, it isn't always an available option. When using cash, it makes your offers easier to accept because there is no financing contingency. Also, you can close faster. As a Realtor, if I receive a financed offer and a cash offer, I will encourage my seller to take the cash offer even if it nets a little less, because there is less chance of things going wrong with a cash offer. In most cases with a cash offer, we only have to get past the inspection period and the title paperwork. Also there is no appraisal or financing contingency to worry about, which makes the transaction less stressful.

Financing

Traditional Financing

There are several banks where you can get a conventional mortgage from a bank to buy a property. The interest rates are the lowest if you choose this route. Typically, your down payment is 20% and your closing costs are 3%–6% of the purchase price. With this kind of financing, you will need to have your own money to do the rehab and you will get the longest terms to pay the loan back. The disadvantage to this kind of loan is that a lot of great deals can't be financed through a traditional bank because of the particular circumstances.

Home Equity Line of Credit or Personal Loan

If you have the equity in your house or can get a personal loan, this is the way to go because, just like cash, it gives you freedom to make offers without a third party involved. You will have to get the loan before you find the property, so you have the money on hand when you purchase the property and do the renovations. The downside to this is that you will have to make payments when the loan funds and you might not even have the property, especially if you took an advance at closing. So, if you go down this route, be sure to already have a property in mind or at least be in the process of looking for the right one.

Private Money Loan (Other People's Money)

I love using other people's money because this means that I can keep mine in my pocket. There are several ways that you can use private money to fund your real estate deals. You can get a hard money loan or you can get a loan from a private investor. Either way, it's a good way to help you acquire real estate without using your own personal money.

Hard Money Loans

A hard money lender is a non-traditional finance company which carries a higher interest rate without the traditional credit requirements for funding.

Advantages

Most loans can close within seven to ten business days.

You will be able to finance the rehab cost as well as the purchase. The normal limits are 75%

LTV(loan to value) while a few select companies offer 90–100% LTV.

These loans are asset-based and based on credit or income, even though most have a minimum credit score requirement.

Typically, you will have interest-only payments for a year.

Disadvantages

If you do get a hard money loan, be prepared for a higher interest rate.

Some of the loans have a balloon payment at the end of the initial twelve-month period (whereas some roll over into a traditional loan).

You have to have money up front to do the rehab in order to request the first draw. This is even the case with the 100% rehab loans.

The lender has to do an appraisal to determine the ARV to make sure that there is enough value in the property in order to lend you the money for the loan.

Private Money Funds

This can be a person or a group of people lending to peers. Normally it just takes a phone call or a handshake to get your deal funded. This is called relationship-based funding. The interest rates might be a little higher than bank financing but the bright side is that the only paperwork is between you, your "lender" and the attorney. Also, there is no qualification process and no appraisal needed.

Business Credit

This is a non-traditional way of acquiring financing but it's credit that you can use time and time again. The programs are credit score driven and you must have an LLC or INC set up with an EIN (tax ID number). The minimum credit score is 700 but the higher yours is, the better. You will acquire several credit cards that give you check writing privileges so you can easily purchase properties. The amount that you acquire will depend on the strength of your credit profile. One thing to remember that this is business credit and it will not affect your personal credit report. In most cases you can acquire several credit lines amounting to up to $250,000 in funding. Because this is a special program, most of the brokers charge a funding fee based on what your approvals are for, so be prepared to pay when you are fully approved. I have several relationships with business credit companies. They have been lifesavers.

Now that you have decided how to acquire the funding, it's time to choose the right team.

Finding the Right Team

Realtor

Whether you are an in state or out of state investor, it is extremely important that you have the right Realtor on your side. All Realtors are not created equal. READ THAT AGAIN! Most Realtors are only as good as what they are given. They are not go-getters and do not want to work hard.

When you are looking for a Realtor, here are some questions to ask.

- How many investors do you currently service?
- What are the best zip codes to purchase properties to achieve the best rental tenants?

- What are the best zip codes to flip properties in?
- What is the average selling time of properties?
- Do you ever come across off-market properties?
- Do you charge to run comps for properties not on the MLS?
- How many properties do you currently have for sale? How long have they been on the market?
- What are the best school zones to purchase in?
- What are customary closing costs? What does the seller pay? What does the buyer pay?
- What type of properties do you normally sell?
- How will you notify me of new properties available for sale?

Of course, this is not an exhaustive list, but it should give you a general idea of what questions to ask a potential Realtor. You want to get to know your Realtor and build a relationship with him or her because, after all, your future is in their hands.

Contractors

Most Realtors have built relationships with several contractors over the years, so ask them for referrals. Now this can backfire on you, in that the Realtor might not be totally honest with you regarding their work ethic — so beware and do your own research. If you are doing a complete rehab, your budget will most likely be over $10,000. In this case you will need a licensed home builder or a licensed general contractor to perform your work. Do you have to go down this route? No, you don't but you should. This is why. Home builders and general contractors are insured, bonded and regulated by the states in which they are licensed. If anything goes wrong then you will have legal recourse. If you choose an unlicensed general contractor, you will not.

Now I bet you are wondering what an unlicensed general contractor is. If you go to the state website and you can't find their name or company, then they are unlicensed. Before you sign any contracts or send any deposits, ask to see a copy of the contractor's state card and their insurance. If they have it then they will be more than happy to send it over to you. If there is any hesitation, RUN!

Things to do before doing business with a contractor:

1. Ask for referrals.
2. Ask for pictures of previous projects.
3. Ask for payment options.
4. Ask for a payment schedule.
5. Find out what happens if they are behind schedule.
6. Find out about their warranty.
7. Get a copy of their business license.
8. Get a copy of their insurance.
9. Ask for a copy of the contract.

Property Management Company

Your property management company can be crucial to your success. A bad property management company is like a bad contractor. If they mismanage your property then it can cost you a lot of money in the end, when you have to make costly repairs.

Questions to ask your property management company:

1. How often they do inspections?
2. Is there a fee for inspections?

3. What forms of payment do they accept for rent payments?
4. How often are owner statements sent out?
5. What are the property management fees?
6. How much is the charge to place a tenant?
7. What happens if the tenant breaks the lease; is there a release fee?
8. How are repairs handled? Are you billed for repairs, or will they be taken out of the rental payments?
9. Who gets the late fees?
10. When are payments considered late?
11. When are late notices issued and how often?
12. When does a tenant get sent an eviction letter?
13. What are the requirements to lease a property?
14. Do they perform a background and employment check when leasing a property?
15. What's the normal timeframe for a property to be leased?

These are the kinds of questions that will start the conversation and hopefully get the other person to start talking. You are looking for someone who is a natural communicator and vice versa. If the conversation starts to sound like an interview, then the other person will get irritated and tune you out. Most of all, please don't sound like a robot, and try to make it personal.

If you follow these steps faithfully and repeat them, your income will grow.

$1 Million Payday

Have you ever wondered how the small She-Vestors can make a million dollars in real estate? I have a twelve-month plan but you have to stay consistent. In order to make $1 million in twelve months, you need to make $83,333 per month. Now, I bet you are looking at this page and saying to yourself that this is impossible, but actually it's not.

You can achieve it in several different ways. Some people find that it is easier to have a partnership because there is less risk involved, while others prefer to do it by themselves. Regardless of how you do it, here is a visual to help you see the road ahead. Below is a chart of the number of properties you need to buy and sell per month, with your potential profit per sale.

# Properties	Profit Per Property
10	$8,333.33
5	$16,666.67
4	$20,833.33
3	$27,777.78
2	$41,666.67

Now I will describe each type of property flip.

Wholesale Flip

This is when you put a property under contract and resell it without doing anything to it. Most of the time you have the property sold before you take possession and you only have title in your name for a day. Examples of wholesale flips are when you make a profit under $10,000. Now, they can make you more profit than that if you have the room to make it work for all parties, so this is just a guideline.

Lipstick Flip

For this type of flip you basically clean up the property. You might perform a trash out (this is when you remove all trash, debris, furniture, etc from the property), along with interior and/or exterior painting, fix cosmetic damage and/or clean up the yard. You make the property appealing to the eye without doing anything structural or major to it. Lipstick flips can often make you between $10,000 and $20,000. Again, this depends on the property value and the type of deal.

Total Renovation Flips

Total renovations are when you do everything possible to get the greatest return. With these flips you can easily make $25,000 or more. In fact, the sky is the limit on these flips.

I personally like wholesale and lipstick flips because they are quick. I figure that I can make basically the same amount of money doing it this way. I will only do a total renovation flip when it makes sense to do so and I don't want to leave that money on the table.

Hindsight is 20/20. Do you recall case study 3 when I sold the quadplex for a $17,500 profit? It seemed like a great idea at the time. If I was thinking properly, I would have invested a little money in the property and I could have at least doubled or tripled my return. Multi-unit properties are rare however, and I wasn't thinking at the time. That would have been a great lipstick flip, had I chosen to do it that way.

Today I am closing on a property for $5,000; it will be a lipstick flip for me. The property is in fairly good condition for the price. I have to do some light plumbing, roof and soffit repairs, perform a trash out, repair the subfloor in two rooms and install Sheetrock in one room. My total renovation costs will be $5,000–$8,000 (I'm allowing for contingencies just in case I decide to make more changes). I will sell this property for around $35,000–$38,000 to another investor, because it will need minimal repairs. When they get it, they will just have to paint and install an HVAC. So, my profit will be about $25,000 less selling costs. Now that's a great payday. I really want to back up a moment; I had contacted the seller of this property in 2019, and made an offer which they accepted verbally then later declined. Then they got back in touch five months later to see if I was still interested. This time I got the property for less than the original offer. Wow! That was awesome!

Do you remember I mentioned the time when I was speaking on systems and I received a phone call from one of my mailers about a property that the caller had bought for her grandson? Well, I went to see the property and it turned out to be an awesome deal. After seeing this property, I decided that this was definitely going to be a flip for me. I really haven't decided if this will be a lipstick or a full renovation flip but it will definitely be a flip. This property has a lot of great potential. The profit potential on it is $45,000–$75,000 depending on which method I use. These are the type of paydays I love!

As you can see from these two examples, the potential profits can be more or less depending on the property. Please don't close this book and only try to look for $5,000 properties, saying you want to put $5,000–$8,000 rehab costs into them expecting that big payday. I promise you that this is a rare occasion. Sometimes you get a great deal and other times you just get a deal. The key is to know how to recognize a great deal when it runs across your path. That will determine your success in this business. Sometimes you will have to spend a little more to make a little less, so just take everything with a grain of salt.

I bet you are wondering why I don't do more retail flips. Honestly, it's because I run across so many good properties where I can make my money by passing them along to the investors that want to do retail flips. It's money for both of us. So, I guess I'm more of an acquisition investor. I go out and do the dirty work for the investor who wants the properties brought to them. I have found that quite a few investors don't want to do a lot of work on properties. They only want to do the basics — so that's where I come in. I can do the heavy lifting for pennies on the dollar which will save them in the long run. It's definitely a win-win for both of us.

I could go on and on about the wonderful deals that I find on a daily basis but I won't. It's a lifestyle for me and I love it. New investors call me every day to see what's on the menu, so to speak. I guess that's why I named this book SHE-VESTOR™ — because that's what I am. The hardest thing about what I do is trying to decide when to keep a property and when to let one go.

The Road Ahead

The road to success is never easy and I didn't say it would be. You will encounter some bumps in the road. Some nights you will get frustrated and wonder if this was all worth it. Other nights you will be dancing around the house thanking God that you didn't give up. Real estate is one of the most lucrative businesses in the world today. Since the beginning of time, some of the wealthiest people have made money in real estate transactions. However, on the flip side, other people have lost everything making bad real estate decisions. Everything in life is a risk and you have to decide what level of risk you are willing to take. When you decide to invest in these properties, whether it's cash or getting a loan, you have to weigh the overall costs.

If you obtain a hard money or private loan, pay close attention to the holding costs, interest rate and loan term. Sometimes it may seem like a good deal when you don't have the money and you can see there is money to be made, however the time frame comes along quick. Anything can happen during a renovation project. Things will not always go as planned. Your contractor can give you an estimate, but they cannot see into the future. Let me further explain. When you are renovating an older house, you may encounter a lot of unknowns including rotten wood, bad floor joists, rotten beams, bad drainage systems, bad sewers etc. A lot of times, there's no way to know these things until the walls are open. You can try to account for these items but it's always next to impossible. So, if you get into a renovation project and your contractor comes back to you requesting more money due to things unforeseen, don't give them a hard time. A good rule of thumb is to make sure that you have at least 10%–20% above the project cost in reserves for the unknowns so that you can finish the project. The worst thing is to start a project and not be able to finish it because you have run out of money.

Have a Plan B in case Plan A doesn't work. Sometimes you can't get the property sold as fast as you want to, so now you have to rent it. Don't be opposed to renting the property. Don't allow the property to sit vacant. This makes the property more susceptible to vandalism. You always have the option of selling the property with tenants in place. Maybe you planned to finance this property 100% on your own but you are running low on money. Be open to getting a partner to help you finish the property up. At that point, it is better to have some cash return than nothing at all. Your options would be to not finish the property and hope to finish on your on with money that you don't have. Or to finish the property with a partner, take a little less profit and get this asset off your books. It can be hard doing this alone, and frightening.

What is your exit strategy? Most people say they have no exit strategy, they plan to keep buying houses. However, that's not true. What happens after you purchase five houses, ten houses? How many do you plan to keep? How long do you plan on keeping them? Do you plan on selling them off to a hedge fund investor once they are fully rented? Do you plan to continue flipping houses for a profit? Do you plan on keeping the properties for a rental income until you retire? Will you leave the properties to your children? It's important to have an exit strategy in place.

This business can be extremely rewarding if it's done right. Just keep your eye on the prize and you will do well.

Conclusion

ongratulations! You made it!! You have just completed the introductory course to real estate investing. Now it's time to advance to the next level and become an expert in this field.

Let's recap. After reading this book, you should have learned:

- How to acquire properties
- How-to carry-on conversations with potential sellers
- How to set a goal
- How to implement systems
- How to find funding
- How to choose a team

Now to perfect yourself in this field, it's import-ant to learn how to close the sale every time. This information is available in my advanced course at www.shevestor.org

At www.shevestor.org you will learn

- Valuable Negotiation Skills
- Closing Techniques
- Contract Etiquette
- How To Get Pass Seller Objectives
- How To Handle Inspections
- How To Acquire Data From The Best Lead Sources
- Private Funding Sources & Hard Money Lenders

I have used these techniques to help me gener-ate $100,000 in the past two months. This income is from only four properties this time versus six properties in four months last year. I can show you how to generate the same type of income and spend less than $1,000 per property on clean up fees. The more you close, the better your skill set becomes.

I have given you the road map, now it's up to you to implement it. If you follow these steps faithfully and repeat them, your income will grow. Remember if you don't make a change, nothing will ever change. Never underestimate yourself when it comes to your ability to go and make something happen. I'm looking forward to meeting other SHE-VESTORS™ along my journey and hope that one day you can tell me your story. Let's go and find more properties so we can create more SHE-VESTOR™ millionaires!

SOMETIMES YOU HAVE TO TAKE A RISK TO CHANGE YOUR LIFE

About the Author

A native of Birmingham, AL, Stephanie graduated from Hueytown High School at the top of her class. After graduation, she attended The University of Alabama at Birmingham where she obtained a Bachelor's of Science Degree in Electrical and Computer Engineering. Stephanie worked in this field for four and a half years until she decided to make a change and enter the real estate world. Throughout her real estate career, she won various awards, always excelling in everything that she did. When she entered real estate, she had a plan to become bigger and better; however, she never knew what that would entail. She took her real estate license and transformed it into an empire with a real estate brokerage (Extreme Agent Inc™) and a renovation and property management company (Syntreme Inc). Stephanie is a licensed Home Builder in the State of Alabama and licensed Real

Estate Broker in Alabama and Georgia. Stephanie, now a real estate veteran with eighteen years' experience, is passing on her knowledge of real estate to you.

www.ingramcontent.com/pod-product-compliance
Lightning Source LLC
Chambersburg PA
CBHW061038050726

47592CB00004B/1493